# Ready-to-Go Reproducibles
# STANDARDIZED TEST SKILL BUILDERS
# TERRANOVA
## Grade 4

New York • Toronto • London • Auckland • Sydney
Mexico City • New Delhi • Hong Kong

Cover design by Kelli Thompson
Interior design by Creative Pages
Interior illustrations by Kate Flanagan

ISBN 0-439-21118-2

# Contents

# Introduction to Teachers

We all know how important it is for students to do well on tests. This book is one in a series designed to help you help your students become better test takers. In the past few years, many statewide tests and national standardized tests have undergone significant changes, not just in *what* they measure but also in *how* they measure content and skills. The examples and practice tests in this book reflect the latest developments in testing, particularly in the CTBS® *TerraNova*. Features include:

- Reading/Language Arts and Math tests organized by themes
- A variety of different types of literature and informational texts
- A combination of multiple-choice and short-answer questions
- Open-ended Math problems with multiple solutions

This book covers the Reading/Language Arts and Math skills tested on the CTBS® *TerraNova* for Grade 4, and it uses the same kinds of test-item formats.

## Practice Tests

There are two Practice Tests in this book, one for Reading/Language Arts and one for Math. Each test is divided into two parts for easy administration. Features of each Practice Test include:

- Sample items for students to work through
- Hints and test-taking tips on how to answer each type of question
- Explanations of the correct answers
- Reminders to help students during an actual test

## Procedures

We recommend that you work through the sample items on each Practice Test with your students. Discuss the questions and how to get the right answers, and then have students take each part of the test. Plan on 25–30 minutes to administer each part of a Practice Test. Have students mark their answers on the test directly, or—for the multiple-choice sections—have students use a copy of the answer sheet on page 44. (For the Math test, students will need a ruler for measuring in inches and in centimeters. The use of calculators is optional but is not recommended.)

Use the Answer Keys at the back of the book to score each test, or have students score the tests themselves. Mark the answer to each item as correct or incorrect. Have students record their scores on a copy of the Scoring Chart (page 48) to help them keep track of their own progress. After each testing session, make sure students have ample opportunity to study their own tests and learn from any mistakes they might have made.

Students who complete the practice tests in this book will become familiar with the kinds of questions they will see on the CTBS® *TerraNova* and other tests, and they will have a new arsenal of techniques and strategies for getting better test scores.

# Reading/Language Arts

## SAMPLES

*Directions*
Read each passage. Choose the best answer to each question.

HINT: Before you read, take a quick look at the questions so you know what to look for in the story.

## Two Friends

One afternoon, two friends were strolling together along a path. Suddenly Melanie bent over and picked up a bag of money that was lying on the grass. "Look what I have found!" she exclaimed. "I'm rich!"

"You should say look what *we* have found," said Lena. "After all, we are friends, and friends should share what they find."

Melanie disagreed. She planned to keep the money for herself.

Soon afterward, Melanie and Lena heard an angry voice yelling after them. "Stop!" cried the man's voice. "There's the thief, officer. She stole my bag."

"Oh, no," said Melanie, "we're in trouble now."

"No," said Lena calmly, "you should say *I* am in trouble, not *we*. You refused to share the prize, so I will not share the punishment."

**A**  **What will most likely happen next?**
  Ⓐ Lena will say that the money is hers.
  Ⓑ The police officer will stop Melanie.
  Ⓒ Lena will say that she stole the money herself.
  Ⓓ Melanie and Lena will run away.

HINT: Look for clues in the story to help figure out the answers.

**B**  **You can tell that Melanie and Lena are most likely in a**
  Ⓕ parking lot       Ⓗ carnival
  Ⓖ bus               Ⓙ park

**C**  **Who yells with the "angry voice"?**
  Ⓐ Melanie                        Ⓒ Lena
  Ⓑ the man who lost the money     Ⓓ the police officer

**D**  **Find the word that best completes the sentence.**
  **The thief jumped over the fence and _____ into the woods.**
  Ⓕ disappear         Ⓗ disappeared
  Ⓖ disappearing      Ⓙ will disappear

Standardized Test Skill Builders—TerraNova, Grade 4

Scholastic Professional Books

# By Gum

HINT: Read the title and the whole passage carefully.

Did you know that kids in North America chew 40 million pieces of bubble gum every day? That's a lot of pink gum! It's a lot of bubbles, too! Bubble gum is so popular that contests are held every year to see who can blow the biggest bubbles. The largest ever blown was 23 inches wide. It was produced by Susan Montgomery Williams of Fresno, California, on July 19, 1994. The bubble was large enough to set a world record. Now you can read about Susan in *The Guinness Book of Records*. You can visit her at her home page on the Internet, too. So far, no one else has matched Susan's <u>feat</u>.

**E** **What is this passage mostly about?**
- Ⓐ Bubble gum is very popular in North America.
- Ⓑ There are millions of kids in North America.
- Ⓒ Bubble-blowing contests are held every year.
- Ⓓ Susan Montgomery Williams won a contest in 1994.

HINT: Look back at the passage to find the answer to each question.

**F** **Susan Williams holds the world record for**
- Ⓕ chewing the most bubble gum
- Ⓖ blowing the most bubbles
- Ⓗ blowing the largest bubble
- Ⓙ collecting bubble-gum wrappers

**G** **You can tell from this passage that <u>feat</u> means**
- Ⓐ a part of the body
- Ⓑ something a person has done
- Ⓒ a large, noisy party
- Ⓓ something that cannot be avoided

**H** **Find the sentence that is complete and is written correctly.**
- Ⓕ She enters many contests.
- Ⓖ A bubble bigger than my head.
- Ⓗ Chewing the gum slowly.
- Ⓙ A pumpkin or maybe a basketball.

**I** **Find three mistakes in the paragraph below. Draw a line through each mistake and write a correction above it.**

> Near the end of July. Krista goed to the mall. She
>
> got some bubble gum. And entered a contest.

**J** **Think about the two passages you have read: "Two Friends" and "By Gum."
Name the most interesting thing you learned from one or both of the passages.**

_____

_____

# Finding the Answers

Questions A-D are about the story "Two Friends." To answer question A, you must predict what will happen next. At the end of the story, an angry man and a police officer are chasing Melanie. They think she is a thief. Based on these clues, the most likely answer is **B**, "The police officer will stop Melanie."

To answer question B, you must look for clues. The story says that Melanie and Lena are walking along a path and the money is lying on the grass, so they are most likely in a park. Answer **J** is correct.

For question C, you must look for clues to help you decide who yells with the "angry voice." The angry person is a man, so it cannot be Melanie or Lena. He is speaking to the officer, so the person is not the police officer. The person says that Melanie stole his bag, so the person who yells must be the man who lost the money, answer **B**.

Question D is about using verbs correctly. The verb you choose should be in the same tense as *jumped*. "The thief *jumped* over the fence and *disappeared* into the woods." The best answer is **H**, "disappeared."

---

## Reading/Language Arts

### SAMPLES

*Directions*
**Read each passage. Choose the best answer to each question.**

> HINT: Before you read, take a quick look at the questions so you know what to look for in the story.

### Two Friends

One afternoon, two friends were strolling together along a path. Suddenly Melanie bent over and picked up a bag of money that was lying on the grass. "Look what I have found!" she exclaimed. "I'm rich!"

"You should say look what *we* have found," said Lena. "After all, we are friends, and friends should share what they find."

Melanie disagreed. She planned to keep the money for herself.

Soon afterward, Melanie and Lena heard an angry voice yelling after them. "Stop!" cried the man's voice. "There's the thief, officer. She stole my bag."

"Oh, no," said Melanie, "we're in trouble now."

"No," said Lena calmly, "you should say *I* am in trouble, not *we*. You refused to share the prize, so I will not share the punishment."

**A** What will most likely happen next?
- Ⓐ Lena will say that the money is hers.
- Ⓑ The police officer will stop Melanie.
- Ⓒ Lena will say that she stole the money herself.
- Ⓓ Melanie and Lena will run away.

> HINT: Look for clues in the story to help figure out the answers.

**B** You can tell that Melanie and Lena are most likely in a
- Ⓕ parking lot
- Ⓖ bus
- Ⓗ carnival
- Ⓙ park

**C** Who yells with the "angry voice"?
- Ⓐ Melanie
- Ⓑ the man who lost the money
- Ⓒ Lena
- Ⓓ the police officer

**D** Find the word that best completes the sentence.
The thief jumped over the fence and _____ into the woods.
- Ⓕ disappear
- Ⓖ disappearing
- Ⓗ disappeared
- Ⓙ will disappear

Standardized Test Skill Builders—TerraNova, Grade 4

---

**Standardized Test Skill Builders—TerraNova, Grade 4**

Scholastic Professional Books

Questions E-H are about the factual article "By Gum." To answer question E, you must decide what the passage is mostly about. The most important idea in a passage is the *main idea*. It may be clearly stated in the passage, or you may have to figure out the main idea from the information given. This passage tells how much bubble gum is chewed every year and how popular the gum is. The correct answer is **A**.

To answer question F, you must find the supporting detail that tells what Susan Williams did to set a world record. Since the passage states that Susan produced the largest bubble ever blown, the correct answer is **H**.

For question G, you must figure out what *feat* means from the way it is used in the passage. The passage says that Susan holds the record for the largest bubble ever blown, and no one else has matched her *feat*. The word *feat* must refer to "something a person has done," answer **B**.

Question H is about writing complete sentences. A complete sentence has a subject, which tells what the sentence is about, and a predicate, which tells what the subject is or does. Answer **F** is correct because it is the only choice that has both a subject (*she*) and a predicate (*enters*).

---

## By Gum

HINT: Read the title and the whole passage carefully.

Did you know that kids in North America chew 40 million pieces of bubble gum every day? That's a lot of pink gum! It's a lot of bubbles, too! Bubble gum is so popular that contests are held every year to see who can blow the biggest bubbles. The largest ever blown was 23 inches wide. It was produced by Susan Montgomery Williams of Fresno, California, on July 19, 1994. The bubble was large enough to set a world record. Now you can read about Susan in *The Guinness Book of Records*. You can visit her at her home page on the Internet, too. So far, no one else has matched Susan's *feat*.

HINT: Look back at the passage to find the answer to each question.

**E**  What is this passage mostly about?
   Ⓐ Bubble gum is very popular in North America.
   Ⓑ There are millions of kids in North America.
   Ⓒ Bubble-blowing contests are held every year.
   Ⓓ Susan Montgomery Williams won a contest in 1994.

**F**  Susan Williams holds the world record for
   Ⓕ chewing the most bubble gum       Ⓗ blowing the largest bubble
   Ⓖ blowing the most bubbles          Ⓙ collecting bubble-gum wrappers

**G**  You can tell from this passage that *feat* means
   Ⓐ a part of the body              Ⓒ a large, noisy party
   Ⓑ something a person has done     Ⓓ something that cannot be avoided

**H**  Find the sentence that is complete and is written correctly.
   Ⓕ She enters many contests.         Ⓗ Chewing the gum slowly.
   Ⓖ A bubble bigger than my head.     Ⓙ A pumpkin or maybe a basketball.

**I**  Find three mistakes in the paragraph below. Draw a line through each mistake and write a correction above it.

   Near the end of July. Krista goed to the mall. She got some bubble gum. And entered a contest.

**J**  Think about the two passages you have read: "Two Friends" and "By Gum." Name the most interesting thing you learned from one or both of the passages.
   _____
   _____

Standardized Test Skill Builders—TerraNova, Grade 4          7

---

In Question I, you must correct three errors in the way the paragraph is written. The example below shows one way to correct the errors.

                              July,        went
   Near the end of ~~July.~~ Krista ~~goed~~ to the mall. She
                    gum and
   got some bubble ~~gum. And~~ entered a contest.

To answer Question J, you must write a sentence telling the most interesting thing you learned from one or both of the passages. For example, you might write that Susan Williams blew a bubble 23 inches wide.

Scholastic Professional Books

# Test-Taking Tips and Reminders for Reading/Language Arts

As you take the Practice Test, try these strategies to help you score better.

✓ Before you read a passage, take a quick look at the questions so you know what to look for in the text.

✓ Read the title and the whole passage carefully.

✓ Look at the picture. Sometimes a picture gives clues to what the passage is about.

✓ To find the main idea, decide what the whole passage is mostly about.

✓ Look for clues in the passage to help answer the questions.

✓ Go back to the passage to find the information you need to answer each question. Key words (such as *who, what, when, where, why, alike,* and *different*) can help you figure out what to look for.

✓ When you draw a conclusion, look for two or more details in the passage to support your answer.

✓ Look for clues in the passage to figure out the meaning of a word you don't know. Then read the answer choices carefully before you choose an answer.

✓ To identify the sequence of events in a passage, look for signal words, such as *first, then, later, finally, next,* and *last.*

✓ For fill-in-the-blank questions, try each answer choice in the blank to see which one makes the most sense.

✓ When you have to write an answer, read the question carefully. Think about how to answer the question before you begin writing. Look for key words in the question to help you decide what your answer should be.

# Reading/Language Arts: Practice Test

## Part 1: Learning From Nature

*Directions*
**This part of the test is about learning from nature.**
**Read each passage. Then choose the best answer to each question.**

# Surviving in the Wilderness

Mr. Ramirez sat on a rock in front of the tent. His sons, Jamie and John, sat beside him. With the tent set up and a pile of firewood ready, they felt prepared for whatever the afternoon would bring.

> **HINT**: Before you read, take a quick look at the questions.

"Now, boys," Mr. Ramirez said, "the important thing about camping in the desert is to be ready for anything. You never know what kind of emergency might come up, so you have to know what to do at all times."

The boys nodded. They wanted to be good campers, and they were eager to learn all they could from their experienced father.

"For example," the father continued, "what would you do if someone fell and broke his leg?"

"Don't move him," Jamie said. "Get him to lie down, in the shade if you can."

"Send someone for help," John added. "Get someone to call for an ambulance."

"Good!" Mr. Ramirez said, grinning. "Very good." He nodded proudly. "But what about this—what would you do if you're camping and you run out of water?"

"Try to find a stream," John said.

"Okay," Mr. Ramirez said, "but let's say you can't find one, and there are no other people around."

The boys thought for a moment. Then they shrugged.

Mr. Ramirez stood up. "Okay, let's go."

The three of them hiked a short distance across the hot sand. Then Mr. Ramirez reached into his backpack and pulled out a mall shovel. He found a level patch of ground and began to dig.

"You're digging a well?" Jamie asked.

"No," Mr. Ramirez answered, "just watch."

He dug a pit about two feet deep and three feet in diameter. Then he put a small paper cup in the middle of the pit. He covered the pit with a dark-green trash bag that he had cut open, and he held the bag in place with some stones around the edges. Then, as his final step, he placed a small rock in the center of the trash bag.

"I don't get it," John said. "All we have is a hole covered with a trash bag."

"Patience," his father answered. "Now we wait."

They sat in the shade of a small scrub tree, dozing lazily in the afternoon heat. Then, after two hours or so, Mr. Ramirez got up. He removed the trash bag from the pit and lifted out the cup, which was half full of water!

The boys were amazed. "How did you do that?" they asked.

"The ground is cool and damp," Mr. Ramirez explained, "even though it might not look it. The sun causes the moisture to evaporate from the ground, and it <u>condenses</u> on the trash bag. Then the droplets trickle down—that's why I put the stone in the center, to give the bag a low point—and they drip into the cup. It doesn't make much, but it will give you emergency water."

Water from the sandy desert! John and Jamie smiled and looked up at their dad. They had a lot to learn.

HINT: Look for clues in the passage to answer each question.

1  **Where were Mr. Ramirez and his sons camping?**
   Ⓐ in the woods     Ⓒ beside a lake
   Ⓑ on a farm     Ⓓ in the desert

2  **Mr. Ramirez dug a pit in the sand to**
   Ⓕ make a trap     Ⓗ build a campfire
   Ⓖ collect water     Ⓙ make a hiding place

3  **Which of these sayings would Mr. Ramirez most likely live by?**
   Ⓐ "The early bird gets the worm."
   Ⓑ "Always be prepared."
   Ⓒ "Don't believe everything you read."
   Ⓓ "Never take risks."

**4**  What did the cup in the pit probably look like?

(F)

(G)

(H)

(J)

**5**  **Which statement about Mr. Ramirez is most likely true?**
 Ⓐ He makes money by inventing things.
 Ⓑ He likes to try new foods.
 Ⓒ He is an elementary school teacher.
 Ⓓ He has been camping many times before.

HINT: Read all the answer choices before you choose one.

**6**  **Mr. Ramirez was teaching his sons how to**
 Ⓕ find food in the wilderness
 Ⓖ take care of themselves
 Ⓗ prepare food over a campfire
 Ⓙ go a long time without water

**7**  **You can tell that when moisture <u>condenses</u>, it**
 Ⓐ turns to water   Ⓒ becomes warmer
 Ⓑ disappears    Ⓓ turns brown

*Directions*
**Choose the word or words that best complete each sentence.**

HINT: Try each answer choice in the blank to see which one makes the most sense.

**8**  **Mr. Ramirez _____ supper for everyone.**
 Ⓕ make    Ⓗ making
 Ⓖ makes    Ⓙ have made

**9**  **Jamie and John _____ brothers.**
 Ⓐ is     Ⓒ being
 Ⓑ was    Ⓓ are

**10**  **Mr. Ramirez and his sons removed the trash bag after they _____ for two hours.**
 Ⓕ wait    Ⓗ had waited
 Ⓖ were waiting  Ⓙ will wait

Scholastic Professional Books

# Frog and Locust

A long time ago, the rain did not come for 12 whole months. The grass turned brown, flowers wilted, and the leaves fell from the trees. In the valley where a river once flowed, only a few puddles remained.

Beside one of those puddles lived a small green frog. The frog watched his puddle <u>shrink</u> just a little each day, and he knew the puddle would soon be gone if rain did not come. That would be the end of the frog.

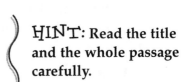

HINT: Read the title and the whole passage carefully.

One morning Frog decided to sing a rain song, and that's what he did. For 15 minutes Frog croaked and croaked, but no rain came. The rain god lived atop a high mountain and could not hear the song.

In a bush nearby lived a small brown locust. The locust knew that if rain did not come soon, he would die, and so the locust sang a rain song, too. For 15 minutes he buzzed and buzzed, but the rain god could not hear him either. When Locust realized that no rain was going to fall, he became so sad that he started to cry.

Frog heard the locust crying and hopped over to the bush. "What's wrong?" asked Frog. When Locust explained what he was crying about, Frog began to cry, too. Together they made quite a racket, and the noise gave Locust an idea.

"Maybe we should sing our songs together," said Locust. Frog immediately agreed, and they began to sing.

With two voices, the rain song was louder than before. But still the sound did not reach the ears of the rain god.

All over the valley, however, other frogs and locusts heard the song. Every frog began to croak, and every locust began to buzz. The creatures sang so loudly that, at last, the rain god heard the song. He gathered up as many dark clouds as he could find, and the rain began to fall.

Soon the river was all filled up again, the trees got their leaves back, and the grass turned green. The world came back to life once more—thanks to Frog and Locust, who decided to join their voices in song.

Scholastic Professional Books

**11** The rain god did not hear Frog and Locust at first because

   Ⓐ he was sleeping

   Ⓑ the rain was too loud

   Ⓒ he was too far away

   Ⓓ the clouds were dark

HINT: Look for clues in the passage to help answer the questions.

**12** At the beginning of the story, what happened to the river?

   Ⓕ It changed course.

   Ⓖ It became dirty.

   Ⓗ It moved away.

   Ⓙ It dried up.

**13** Frog and Locust "made quite a racket" means that they

   Ⓐ made a lot of noise

   Ⓑ had a good life

   Ⓒ made a lot of money

   Ⓓ lived happily ever after

**14** You would be most likely to find this story in

   Ⓕ a newspaper

   Ⓖ a collection of folktales

   Ⓗ a science textbook

   Ⓙ an encyclopedia

**15** The frog watched his puddle <u>shrinking</u> a little each day. Which word means the *opposite* of <u>shrink</u>?

   Ⓐ dry

   Ⓑ wilt

   Ⓒ move

   Ⓓ grow

**16** What lesson can be learned from this story?

   Ⓕ Working together is better than working alone.

   Ⓖ People who try too hard usually fail.

   Ⓗ Good things come to those who wait.

   Ⓙ Animals and people do not get along.

**17** **Which of these is a complete sentence?**
    Ⓐ Many frogs living in the pond.
    Ⓑ A colorful fish in the water.
    Ⓒ Two large frogs rested on a log.
    Ⓓ Peeping and croaking all night long.

HINT: Read all the answer choices before you choose one.

*Directions*
**For questions 18 and 19, choose the sentence that is written correctly.**

**18**     Ⓕ Raquel and I met last year at a Summer Camp.
    Ⓖ Raquel is from brazil, and I'm from new york.
    Ⓗ We shared a cabin and get to know each other really well.
    Ⓙ This year we won't be sharing a cabin, but we'll still be friends.

**19**     Ⓐ Claire wants to be a scientist someday.
    Ⓑ Her and Mary went to the science museum.
    Ⓒ Claire and her friend both likes to study plants.
    Ⓓ Everybody are going on a field trip next week.

**20** **Find the sentence that best combines these two sentences into one.**

**Derek loves camping.**
**Derek doesn't enjoy hiking.**
    Ⓕ Derek loves camping, and he doesn't enjoy hiking.
    Ⓖ Derek loves camping, he doesn't enjoy hiking.
    Ⓗ Derek loves camping, but he doesn't enjoy hiking.
    Ⓙ Derek loves camping or doesn't enjoy hiking.

# Let's Write

Write your answer to each of these questions about "Surviving in the Wilderness" and "Frog and Locust."

**21**   In "Frog and Locust," why did Frog and Locust feel sad?

_____

_____

HINT: Read each question carefully. Think about how to answer the question before you begin writing.

**22**   In "Surviving in the Wilderness," how did Jamie and John feel at first about the pit in the ground? How did they feel at the end?

At first, they _____

_____

At the end, they _____

_____

**23**   Name one way in which these two stories are alike.

_____

_____

_____

**24** Here is a letter that Jamie Ramirez wrote. Find five mistakes in grammar, capitalization, and punctuation. Draw a line through each mistake. Above the line, write the word or words correctly.

Dear Andy,

I will be leaving Uncle Bobs house tomorrow. Dad and me are going to cooperstown, new york. Going to visit the Baseball Hall of Fame.

your friend.

Jamie

**25** What is the most interesting thing you learned from reading "Surviving in the Wilderness" and "Frog and Locust"? Write one interesting thing you learned. (Be sure to use complete sentences and check your answer for correct spelling, capitalization, and punctuation.)

_____

_____

_____

_____

_____

_____

# Reading/Language Arts: Practice Test

## Part 2: Taking Flight

### Directions

This part of the test is about flying—in a hot-air balloon and in outer space. Read each passage. Then choose the best answer to each question.

> HINT: Before you read the passage, take a quick look at the questions so you know what to look for.

# Up, Up, and Away

On February 22, 2000, balloonist Kevin Uliassi lifted off from Loves Park, Illinois. His hot-air balloon was named the *J. Renee*, after his wife. His goal was to be the first person to travel solo around the world in a balloon.

Kevin Uliassi, 36, is an engineer. He lives in Scottsdale, Arizona, and has been flying since he was 17 years old. When he took off in the *J. Renee*, he hoped to fulfill a lifelong dream.

After launching from Illinois, Kevin flew east across the United States. When he reached the Atlantic Ocean, he turned south. Then, from the Caribbean Sea, he turned east again and headed for Africa.

For much of the trip, Kevin flew at an altitude of 20,000 to 30,000 feet. At that altitude, the air is so thin that he had to have oxygen tanks on board to help him breathe.

On February 28, six days into the trip, Kevin and his balloon reached Africa. After several days of flying over the Atlantic Ocean, it was a great relief to be flying over land again. Kevin crossed the African continent and the Middle East. Then he flew across India and headed toward Southeast Asia.

On March 3, Kevin faced his first serious problem. His oxygen system was not working properly. When he could not fix the system himself, Kevin realized that he would have to land.

After traveling more than 13,000 miles and going more than halfway around the world, Kevin landed in the Asian country of Myanmar, which used to be called Burma. He was rescued by local people and reported that he felt fine.

It was too bad that Kevin Uliassi did not complete his trip around the world. But he did set a world record for flying solo in a balloon. He was in the air for ten days, three hours, and 46 minutes. That was about one and a half days longer than the previous record.

**26** **What is the main idea of this passage?**
  F  Kevin's balloon was named after his wife.
  G  Kevin Uliassi tried to fly solo around the world in a balloon.
  H  Kevin has been flying since he was 17.
  J  Kevin Uliassi lifted off from Loves Park, Illinois, on February 22, 2000.

HINT: To find the main idea, decide what the whole passage is mostly about.

**27** **After leaving the United States, what land did Kevin reach next?**
  A  Africa
  B  the Middle East
  C  India
  D  Southeast Asia

**28** **How is the air at 20,000 feet different from the air at ground level?**
  F  It is thicker.
  G  It has more moisture.
  H  It is heavier.
  J  It has less oxygen.

HINT: To find an opinion, look for the sentence that expresses a feeling or belief.

**29** **Which sentence states an opinion?**
  A  Kevin Uliassi is an engineer.
  B  It was too bad that Kevin Uliassi did not complete his trip.
  C  Kevin Uliassi landed in the Asian country of Myanmar.
  D  On February 28, six days into the trip, Kevin reached Africa.

**30** **Which detail supports the idea that Kevin Uliassi was an experienced balloonist?**
  F  He hoped to fulfill a lifelong dream.
  G  He is an engineer.
  H  He has been flying since he was 17.
  J  He could not fix the oxygen system himself.

Standardized Test Skill Builders—TerraNova, Grade 4

Scholastic Professional Books

**31** What was Kevin's most serious problem?

    Ⓐ His balloon drifted off course.

    Ⓑ He flew through a rainstorm.

    Ⓒ His oxygen system stopped working.

    Ⓓ He landed in Myanmar.

HINT: Look for clues in the passage to answer each question.

**32** The passage says, "He hoped to <u>fulfill</u> a lifelong dream." The word <u>fulfill</u> means

    Ⓕ satisfy

    Ⓖ create

    Ⓗ relive

    Ⓙ change

*Directions*

Read this paragraph about Antarctica to answer questions 33 and 34.

_____ (1) It is covered by a sheet of ice a mile thick. (2) Very few animals live there because it's too cold. (3) Parts of Russia are also very cold. (4) The only people who live in Antarctica are scientists.

**33** Which is the best topic sentence for this paragraph?

    Ⓐ Spring begins in October in Antarctica.

    Ⓑ Richard Byrd made five trips to Antarctica.

    Ⓒ Some penguins live in Antarctica, but many live in warmer places.

    Ⓓ Antarctica is the coldest place on Earth.

**34** Which sentence does <u>not</u> belong in this paragraph?

    Ⓕ Sentence 1

    Ⓖ Sentence 2

    Ⓗ Sentence 3

    Ⓙ Sentence 4

**35** Find the sentence that is complete and is written correctly.

    Ⓐ Crossed the frozen sea.

    Ⓑ He traveled by dogsled.

    Ⓒ Many signs of danger.

    Ⓓ Icebergs floating in the water.

HINT: Read the title and the whole passage carefully.

# Living in Space

Shannon Lucid was born on January 14, 1943, in Shanghai, China. At the time, China was fighting in World War II. When Shannon was just six weeks old, she and her American parents were placed in a Japanese prison camp. They were let go a year later and returned to the United States, where they settled in Bethany, Oklahoma.

When she was a young girl, Lucid came across a book that helped decide her future. The book was about Robert Goddard, a pioneer in the building of rockets. After reading about Goddard, Lucid knew what she wanted to do.

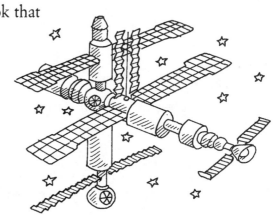

Shannon Lucid had a real love for space and science. She learned to fly an airplane when she was 20. She also went to the University of Oklahoma to study science. In 1973, when NASA announced that it was looking for women to become astronauts, Lucid signed up right away. She was <u>selected</u> by NASA in January 1978. Lucid was one of the first six American women ever chosen for astronaut training. She became an astronaut in August 1979.

Lucid is a scientist who loves flying. When she was invited to live and work on *Mir*, a Russian space station, it was like a dream come true. Lucid had a lot of work to do to get ready, though. First, she had to learn to speak Russian. Then, she had to learn all about the space station where she would be living with two Russian cosmonauts. On March 22, 1996, Lucid lifted off from Kennedy Space Center and headed for the *Mir* space station.

Living in a space station 240 miles above the earth can get pretty boring. How did Lucid pass the time? She spent many hours doing science experiments. She also sent e-mail every day to her husband and grown children, and she read close to 50 books.

Lucid's mission on *Mir* was scheduled to last four and a half months. However, because of bad weather and other problems, she had to stay six weeks longer. She returned to Earth on September 26, 1996. At age 53, Dr. Shannon Lucid had made history. She had spent 188 days in space—an American record.

Upon her safe return, Dr. Lucid was honored by President Bill Clinton. The President called her achievement "a monument to the human spirit." She was awarded a Space Medal of Honor in December 1996.

**36** **What is this selection mostly about?**
F the Russian space station
G Shannon Lucid's career
H the Space Medal of Honor
J Shannon Lucid's parents

HINT: Go back to the passage to find the information you need.

**37** **What kind of selection is this?**
A science fiction
B folktale
C historical fiction
D biography

**38** **Which word best describes Dr. Lucid?**
F adventurous
G caring
H fearful
J restless

**39** **What did Lucid do first to prepare for her mission on *Mir*?**
A She lifted off from Kennedy Space Center.
B She sent e-mail to her family.
C She learned to speak Russian.
D She learned to fly an airplane.

HINT: To identify the sequence of events, look for signal words and dates.

**40** **Lucid was** <u>selected</u> **by NASA to become an astronaut. Which word means the same as** <u>selected</u>**?**
F trained
G encouraged
H discovered
J chosen

**41** **In 1996, Dr. Lucid set the American record for**
A number of books read by an astronaut
B fastest speed in a spaceship
C number of days spent in space
D most problems on a space flight

Scholastic Professional Books

## Directions

For questions 42 and 43, choose the answer that uses correct capitalization and punctuation.

> The first space shuttle was launched on   (42)  . Shuttles are launched from the Kennedy Space Center near   (43)  .

**42**
  Ⓕ April 12 1981
  Ⓖ April 12, 1981
  Ⓗ april 12 1981
  Ⓙ april 12, 1981

**43**
  Ⓐ Orlando Florida
  Ⓑ Orlando, florida
  Ⓒ orlando florida
  Ⓓ Orlando, Florida

## Directions

For questions 44 and 45, choose the correct spelling of the word to complete each sentence.

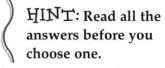

HINT: Read all the answers before you choose one.

**44** My uncle is a _____ for World Airways.
  Ⓕ pilot      Ⓗ pilote
  Ⓖ pillot     Ⓙ pilate

**45** He _____ an award for his safety record.
  Ⓐ recieved     Ⓒ reseeved
  Ⓑ received     Ⓓ reseved

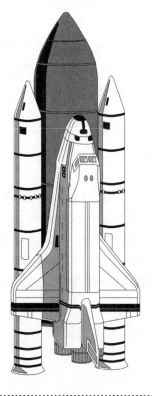

# Let's Write

Write your answer to each of these questions about "Up, Up, and Away" and "Living in Space."

**46**  In "Up, Up, and Away," what was Kevin Uliassi's goal?

_____

_____

**47**  Why didn't Kevin Uliassi reach his goal? Explain.

_____

_____

HINT: Read each question carefully. Look for key words to help you decide what your answer should be.

**48**  According to "Living in Space," why did Shannon Lucid have to learn to speak Russian?

_____

_____

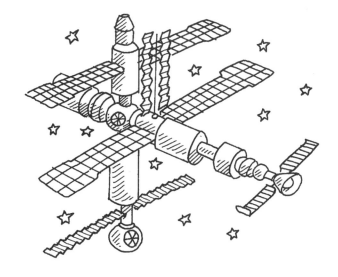

**49** Here is a paragraph written by a student. Find five mistakes in grammar, capitalization, and punctuation. Draw a line through each mistake. Above the line, write the word or words correctly.

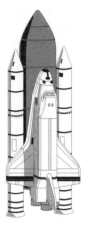

The first airplane flights take place on December 17

1903. Orville and wilbur wright made history that day in Kitty

Hawk, north carolina. Each man made two flights. The most

long flight lasted 59 seconds.

**50** If you had the chance, would you rather fly in a hot-air balloon or on the Space Shuttle? Tell why. (Be sure to use complete sentences and check your answer for correct spelling, capitalization, and punctuation.)

HINT: Check your work.

_____

_____

_____

_____

_____

_____

# Mathematics

## SAMPLES

HINT: Read each problem carefully.

*Directions*

Choose the best answer to each question. If your answer is not given, mark "None of these."

**A** Tanya had 35 comic books. She gave 7 comic books to a friend. How many did she have left?

   Ⓐ 42

   Ⓑ 38

   Ⓒ 32

   Ⓓ 28

   Ⓔ None of these

HINT: Look for key words and numbers to help solve each problem.

**B** Clem has to make a picture showing $\frac{5}{8}$. Which of these figures has $\frac{5}{8}$ shaded?

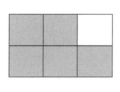 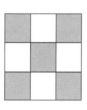 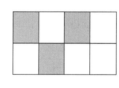 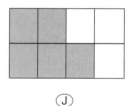

   Ⓕ        Ⓖ        Ⓗ        Ⓙ

**C** There are 78 girls and 91 boys at a summer camp. Which numbers give the best estimate of the total number of children at the camp?

   Ⓐ 70 + 90

   Ⓑ 70 + 100

   Ⓒ 80 + 90

   Ⓓ 80 + 100

**D** Kate is going to a movie that starts at 4:15. According to the clock, how much time does she have before the movie begins?

- Ⓕ 10 minutes
- Ⓖ 15 minutes
- Ⓗ 25 minutes
- Ⓙ 30 minutes
- Ⓚ None of these

**E** Terrell needs 65 cents to pay for a snack. He has only quarters, dimes, and nickels. Show three different ways he could make 65 cents.

| | | |
|---|---|---|
| | | |

Scholastic Professional Books

# Finding the Answers

To answer question A, you must decide whether to add, subtract, multiply, or divide. As you read the problem, look for key words and numbers. Tanya had 35 comic books and gave 7 to a friend. To find *how many she had left*, you must subtract: $35 - 7 = 28$. Answer **D** is correct.

In question B, you must find the figure that has a total of eight parts with five of them shaded. Answer F cannot be correct because the figure has six parts. The figure in answer G has nine parts. The figures in answers H and J have eight parts each, but only the figure in answer J has five of the eight parts shaded. Answer **J** is correct.

To answer question C, you need to choose the numbers that will give the best estimate for 78 + 91. To find an estimate, round each number to the nearest 10. In this problem, the best estimate would be 80 + 90. Answer **C** is correct.

Question D involves telling time. The clock shows that the time is 3:55 (or 5 minutes before 4:00), and the movie begins at 4:15. To find how much time Kate has before the movie begins, you can count the minutes on the clock from 3:55 to 4:15, or you can add: 5 minutes

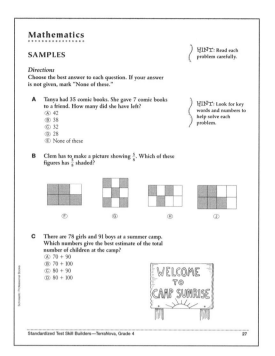

(before 4:00) + 15 minutes (after 4:00) = 20 minutes. Since "20 minutes" is not one of the answers given, you would mark answer **K**, "None of these."

In question E, you need to draw or write three different ways to make 65 cents using only quarters, dimes, and nickels. There are many different combinations of coins that will add up to 65 cents. The picture below shows three possible answers.

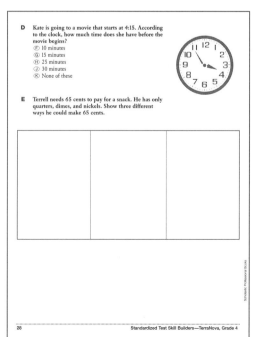

20 Minutes

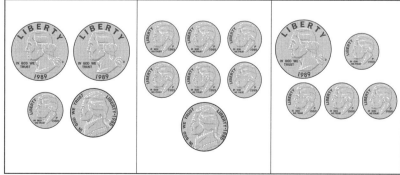

# Test-Taking Tips and Reminders for Mathematics

As you take the Practice Test, try these strategies to help you score better.

✓ Read each problem carefully to make sure you know what it is asking for.

✓ Look for key words to help you decide whether you should add, subtract, multiply, or divide.

✓ Write a number sentence to help you solve each problem.

✓ Always rewrite fractions in their simplest form.

✓ To add or subtract decimals, be sure to line up the decimal points.

✓ Try each answer choice to find the one that is correct.

✓ Eliminate any answers that you know are wrong. Then, if you are still not sure of the answer, make your best guess.

✓ To estimate, round each number to the nearest 10 or 100.

✓ Check your work to make sure you have computed correctly.

✓ Look back at the table, chart, or graph to find the information you need for each question.

✓ Draw your own picture if it will help you solve the problem.

✓ Check your answer to be sure it makes sense.

Scholastic Professional Books

# Mathematics: Practice Test

## Part 1

*Directions*

Choose the best answer to each question. If your answer is not given, mark "None of these."

The fourth graders at Sanderson School are building a puppet theater and planning to put on a show. Do Numbers 1 through 6 about the puppet theater.

**1** A total of 110 people will come to the puppet show. So far, the students have set up 68 chairs. How many more chairs should they set up to seat 110 people?

Ⓐ 32
Ⓑ 38
Ⓒ 42
Ⓓ 48
Ⓔ None of these

**HINT**: Look for key words to help you decide how to solve the problem.

**2** Jesse has cut four pieces of foam board to use for the theater. Which two pieces are the same size and shape?

Ⓕ 1 and 3
Ⓖ 3 and 4
Ⓗ 1 and 4
Ⓙ 2 and 3
Ⓚ None of these

  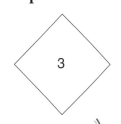 

**3** Martha has $\frac{7}{8}$ of a yard of fabric to make a curtain for the theater. If she uses $\frac{5}{8}$ of a yard, how much fabric will be left over?

Ⓐ $\frac{1}{8}$ yard
Ⓑ $\frac{1}{4}$ yard
Ⓒ $\frac{1}{2}$ yard
Ⓓ $1\frac{1}{2}$ yards
Ⓔ None of these

**HINT**: Always rewrite fractions in their simplest form.

**4** There are 32 students in the class. The teacher wants to split them into 4 equal groups. Which number sentence should she use to find the number of students in each group?

Ⓕ $32 + 4 = \square$

Ⓖ $32 - 4 = \square$

Ⓗ $32 \times 4 = \square$

Ⓙ $32 \div 4 = \square$

Ⓚ None of these

**5** Landon made 4.3 feet of blue trim and 2.9 feet of gold trim for the theater. How many feet of trim did he make all together?

Ⓐ 1.4 feet

Ⓑ 6.2 feet

Ⓒ 6.3 feet

Ⓓ 7.3 feet

Ⓔ None of these

HINT: Read each problem carefully to make sure you know what it is asking for.

**6** For the puppet show, $\frac{2}{3}$ of the puppets are animals. Which figure shows $\frac{2}{3}$ shaded?

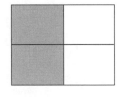

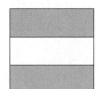

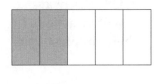

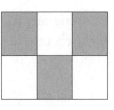

Scholastic Professional Books

Each spring the fourth-grade students in Ms. Holliday's class hold a plant sale. Do Numbers 7–15 about the plant sale.

**7** A seed tray has 4 rows with 8 cups in each row. Which number sentence shows the total number of cups in the tray?

Ⓐ $8 + 4 = \square$

Ⓑ $8 - 4 = \square$

Ⓒ $8 \times 4 = \square$

Ⓓ $8 \div 4 = \square$

**8** Nina checked the temperature in the gym where the sale was held. What was the temperature?

Ⓕ 50°F

Ⓖ 53°F

Ⓗ 55°F

Ⓙ 56°F

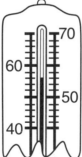

**9** Mrs. Keller bought a plant from Susan for $4.25. She gave Susan $10.00. How much change should Susan give her?

Ⓐ $5.75

Ⓑ $6.25

Ⓒ $6.75

Ⓓ $14.25

HINT: Write a number sentence to help you solve each problem.

For Numbers 10–12, use the bar graph showing the number of plants sold on each day of the sale.

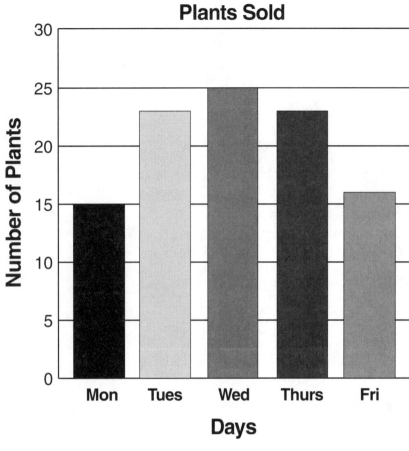

**Plants Sold**

HINT: Look back at the graph to find the information you need for each question.

**10** On which day were the fewest plants sold?
Ⓕ Monday
Ⓖ Tuesday
Ⓗ Thursday
Ⓙ Friday

**11** How many more plants were sold on Thursday than on Friday?
Ⓐ 6
Ⓑ 7
Ⓒ 16
Ⓓ 23

**12** What was the greatest number of plants sold in one day?
Ⓕ 15 plants
Ⓖ 20 plants
Ⓗ 23 plants
Ⓙ 25 plants

Standardized Test Skill Builders—TerraNova, Grade 4

Scholastic Professional Books

**13**   How tall is the seedling? Use a centimeter ruler.

    Ⓐ 4 cm

    Ⓑ 4 $\frac{1}{2}$ cm

    Ⓒ 5 cm

    Ⓓ 45 cm

> **HINT:** Read the problem carefully to make sure you know what it is asking for.

**14**   Hans worked at the plant sale on Friday. He sold an average of 3 plants per hour. What else do you need to know to find the total number of plants Hans sold on Friday?

    Ⓕ the price of each plant

    Ⓖ how many hours he worked

    Ⓗ how many customers came in

    Ⓙ how much money he collected

**15**   Sharon is making a paper chain with the pattern shown below. If this pattern continues, which shape should come next?

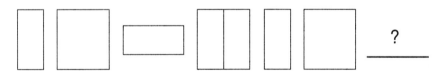

*Directions*

Write or draw your answer to each question.

**16** Melanie wants to buy a key chain that costs $0.76. She has quarters, dimes, nickels, and pennies. Show three ways that she could pay exactly $0.76.

|  |  |  |
|--|--|--|
|  |  |  |

**17** On the lines below, write a word problem that uses addition or multiplication. The answer to your problem should be "42 baseball cards."

HINT: Check your answer to be sure it makes sense.

_____

_____

_____

_____

**18** Show how to solve your word problem using numbers.

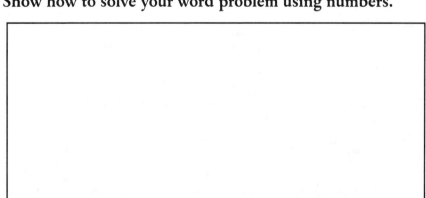

Standardized Test Skill Builders—TerraNova, Grade 4

Scholastic Professional Books

**19**   Jenny rolls 5 number cubes and gets the numbers shown.

Then she arranges them to make a 5-digit number. What is the greatest possible 5-digit number she can make? Write the number and explain how you made it.

}  HINT: Draw your own picture if it will help you solve a problem.

_____

_____

_____

_____

**20**   Janice made a spinner for the game she is playing with Jack. Are the odds of spinning an A, a B, or a C the same?

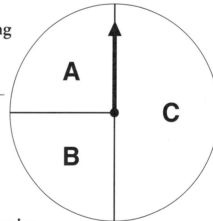

_____

If the odds are not the same, what could Janice do to make the odds of getting each letter the same? Explain.

_____

_____

_____

_____

Scholastic Professional Books

# Mathematics: Practice Test

## Part 2

*Directions*
Choose the best answer to each question. If your
answer is not given, mark "None of these."

HINT: Check your
work to make sure you
have computed
correctly.

**21**
$$\begin{array}{r} 115 \\ 321 \\ + 676 \\ \hline \end{array}$$

    Ⓐ 1001
    Ⓑ 1011
    Ⓒ 1111
    Ⓓ 1112
    Ⓔ None of these

**22**   $112 \times 2 =$
    Ⓕ 114
    Ⓖ 124
    Ⓗ 204
    Ⓙ 214
    Ⓚ None of these

**23**
$$\begin{array}{r} 6.7 \\ - 0.4 \\ \hline \end{array}$$

    Ⓐ 6.3
    Ⓑ 6.11
    Ⓒ 7.1
    Ⓓ 10.7
    Ⓔ None of these

**24**   $\dfrac{1}{6} + \dfrac{5}{6} =$
    Ⓕ $\dfrac{1}{2}$
    Ⓖ $\dfrac{6}{12}$
    Ⓗ 1
    Ⓙ $\dfrac{4}{6}$
    Ⓚ None of these

Each February the fourth-grade class at Jones Elementary School runs a post office for the whole school. Do Numbers 25 through 31 about the post office.

**25**  Maggie was standing in line at the school post office to buy stamps. Exactly five students were in front of her. What was her place in line?

(A) first
(B) fourth
(C) fifth
(D) sixth

**26**  One kind of stamp has an even number on it.
Which of these could be the number?

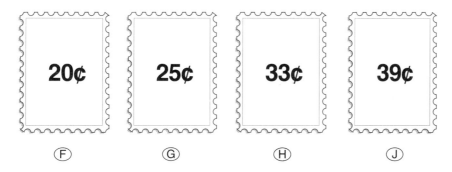

| | | | |
|---|---|---|---|
| 20¢ | 25¢ | 33¢ | 39¢ |
| (F) | (G) | (H) | (J) |

**27**  The post office opens each day at 11:45 A.M. and closes at 2:15 P.M. How long is the post office open each day?

(A) 1 hour, 30 minutes
(B) 2 hours, 15 minutes
(C) 2 hours, 30 minutes
(D) 3 hours

**28**  During the month, the class sold 1,361 stamps. What is this number rounded to the nearest hundred?

(F) 1,000
(G) 1,300
(H) 1,400
(J) 2,000

**HINT:** Eliminate any answers that you know are wrong. Then make your best guess.

**29**  Four students made up designs for their own stamps.
In which design is the dotted line a line of symmetry?

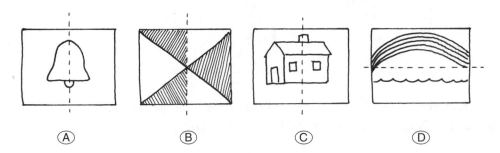

**30**  When D.J. gets to the post office, he looks
at the clock. What time does the clock show?

   (F) 11:15
   (G) 12:20
   (H) 1:20
   (J) 4:00

**31**  A student made a map of the neighborhood near the
Jones School. Which streets on the map are parallel?

   (A) Pine and Spring
   (B) Corley and Pine
   (C) Spring and Lake
   (D) Lake and Corley

HINT: Look at the
picture or diagram
carefully.

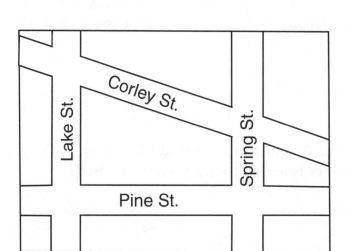

Scholastic Professional Books

# Class Trip

Mr. Johnson's class is planning a day trip to Spring Mill Park. Do Numbers 32–35 about the trip.

**32** It takes about 20 minutes to drive from the school to the park. Which unit should be used to measure the distance between the school and the park?

 Ⓕ grams
 Ⓖ kilometers
 Ⓗ pounds
 Ⓙ centimeters

> **HINT:** Try each answer choice to find the one that is correct.

**33** The trip is planned for a Friday in March. Which of these could be the date of the trip?

 Ⓐ March 18
 Ⓑ March 19
 Ⓒ March 20
 Ⓓ March 25

| MARCH | | | | | | |
|---|---|---|---|---|---|---|
| SUN | MON | TUE | WED | THU | FRI | SAT |
| | 1 | 2 | 3 | 4 | 5 | 6 |
| 7 | 8 | 9 | 10 | 11 | 12 | 13 |
| 14 | 15 | 16 | 17 | 18 | 19 | 20 |
| 21 | 22 | 23 | 24 | 25 | 26 | 27 |
| 28 | 29 | 30 | 31 | | | |

**34** Hannah brought a rectangular picnic blanket that is 6 feet long and 5 feet wide. What area will the blanket cover?

 Ⓕ 11 square feet
 Ⓖ 25 square feet
 Ⓗ 30 square feet
 Ⓙ 36 square feet

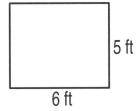

**35** Food is packed in a box that is 4 units long, 3 units wide, and 2 units high. What is the volume of the box?

 Ⓐ 9 cubic units
 Ⓑ 11 cubic units
 Ⓒ 14 cubic units
 Ⓓ 24 cubic units

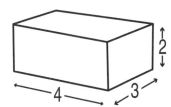

*Directions*

Write or draw your answer to each question.

**36** A school group is going to the science museum. Tickets for the museum cost $4.00 for each adult and $2.00 for each student. The group spends a total of $68.00 for tickets. How many adults and how many students could be in the group? Find two different combinations of adults and students. Show your work.

 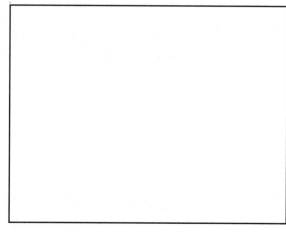

**37** A total of 82 people go to the Fourth of July barbecue in Roseville. Each person pays $4.85 for lunch. <u>About</u> how much money is collected for the barbecue? Estimate your answer and explain how you estimated.

_____

_____

_____

**38** A rectangular garden is 20 feet long and 5 feet wide. What is the perimeter of the garden? Show your work.

HINT: Check your answer to be sure it makes sense.

5 ft

20 ft

Standardized Test Skill Builders—TerraNova, Grade 4

Scholastic Professional Books

**39** Trish has three T-shirts. One is red, one is yellow, and one is green. She has two pairs of shorts, one black and one white. How many different outfits of one T-shirt and one pair of shorts can Trish make? Show your work.

}HINT: Read each problem carefully to make sure you know what it is asking for.

**40** Moira asked all the students in her class how they got to school. She wrote the results on a notepad. Using Moira's tally, make a bar graph on the grid below to show the results of Moira's survey. (Be sure to include a title and labels.)

| Bus | ‖‖‖ ‖‖‖ ‖ |
|------|------------|
| Car | ‖‖‖ ‖‖‖ |
| Walk | ‖‖‖ |
| Bike | ‖‖‖ ‖ |

# ANSWER SHEET

Student Name _____ Grade _____

Teacher Name _____ Date _____

## Reading/Language Arts Samples

A Ⓐ Ⓑ Ⓒ Ⓓ    E Ⓐ Ⓑ Ⓒ Ⓓ
B Ⓕ Ⓖ Ⓗ Ⓙ    F Ⓕ Ⓖ Ⓗ Ⓙ
C Ⓐ Ⓑ Ⓒ Ⓓ    G Ⓐ Ⓑ Ⓒ Ⓓ
D Ⓕ Ⓖ Ⓗ Ⓙ    H Ⓕ Ⓖ Ⓗ Ⓙ

## Mathematics Samples

A Ⓐ Ⓑ Ⓒ Ⓓ Ⓔ
B Ⓕ Ⓖ Ⓗ Ⓙ Ⓚ
C Ⓐ Ⓑ Ⓒ Ⓓ Ⓔ
D Ⓕ Ⓖ Ⓗ Ⓙ Ⓚ

## Practice Test, Part 1

1 Ⓐ Ⓑ Ⓒ Ⓓ
2 Ⓕ Ⓖ Ⓗ Ⓙ
3 Ⓐ Ⓑ Ⓒ Ⓓ
4 Ⓕ Ⓖ Ⓗ Ⓙ
5 Ⓐ Ⓑ Ⓒ Ⓓ
6 Ⓕ Ⓖ Ⓗ Ⓙ
7 Ⓐ Ⓑ Ⓒ Ⓓ
8 Ⓕ Ⓖ Ⓗ Ⓙ
9 Ⓐ Ⓑ Ⓒ Ⓓ
10 Ⓕ Ⓖ Ⓗ Ⓙ
11 Ⓐ Ⓑ Ⓒ Ⓓ
12 Ⓕ Ⓖ Ⓗ Ⓙ
13 Ⓐ Ⓑ Ⓒ Ⓓ
14 Ⓕ Ⓖ Ⓗ Ⓙ
15 Ⓐ Ⓑ Ⓒ Ⓓ
16 Ⓕ Ⓖ Ⓗ Ⓙ
17 Ⓐ Ⓑ Ⓒ Ⓓ
18 Ⓕ Ⓖ Ⓗ Ⓙ
19 Ⓐ Ⓑ Ⓒ Ⓓ
20 Ⓕ Ⓖ Ⓗ Ⓙ

## Practice Test, Part 2

26 Ⓕ Ⓖ Ⓗ Ⓙ
27 Ⓐ Ⓑ Ⓒ Ⓓ
28 Ⓕ Ⓖ Ⓗ Ⓙ
29 Ⓐ Ⓑ Ⓒ Ⓓ
30 Ⓕ Ⓖ Ⓗ Ⓙ
31 Ⓐ Ⓑ Ⓒ Ⓓ
32 Ⓕ Ⓖ Ⓗ Ⓙ
33 Ⓐ Ⓑ Ⓒ Ⓓ
34 Ⓕ Ⓖ Ⓗ Ⓙ
35 Ⓐ Ⓑ Ⓒ Ⓓ
36 Ⓕ Ⓖ Ⓗ Ⓙ
37 Ⓐ Ⓑ Ⓒ Ⓓ
38 Ⓕ Ⓖ Ⓗ Ⓙ
39 Ⓐ Ⓑ Ⓒ Ⓓ
40 Ⓕ Ⓖ Ⓗ Ⓙ
41 Ⓐ Ⓑ Ⓒ Ⓓ
42 Ⓕ Ⓖ Ⓗ Ⓙ
43 Ⓐ Ⓑ Ⓒ Ⓓ
44 Ⓕ Ⓖ Ⓗ Ⓙ
45 Ⓐ Ⓑ Ⓒ Ⓓ

## Practice Test, Part 1

1 Ⓐ Ⓑ Ⓒ Ⓓ Ⓔ
2 Ⓕ Ⓖ Ⓗ Ⓙ Ⓚ
3 Ⓐ Ⓑ Ⓒ Ⓓ Ⓔ
4 Ⓕ Ⓖ Ⓗ Ⓙ Ⓚ
5 Ⓐ Ⓑ Ⓒ Ⓓ Ⓔ
6 Ⓕ Ⓖ Ⓗ Ⓙ Ⓚ
7 Ⓐ Ⓑ Ⓒ Ⓓ Ⓔ
8 Ⓕ Ⓖ Ⓗ Ⓙ Ⓚ
9 Ⓐ Ⓑ Ⓒ Ⓓ Ⓔ
10 Ⓕ Ⓖ Ⓗ Ⓙ Ⓚ
11 Ⓐ Ⓑ Ⓒ Ⓓ Ⓔ
12 Ⓕ Ⓖ Ⓗ Ⓙ Ⓚ
13 Ⓐ Ⓑ Ⓒ Ⓓ Ⓔ
14 Ⓕ Ⓖ Ⓗ Ⓙ Ⓚ
15 Ⓐ Ⓑ Ⓒ Ⓓ Ⓔ

## Practice Test, Part 2

21 Ⓕ Ⓖ Ⓗ Ⓙ Ⓚ
22 Ⓐ Ⓑ Ⓒ Ⓓ Ⓔ
23 Ⓕ Ⓖ Ⓗ Ⓙ Ⓚ
24 Ⓐ Ⓑ Ⓒ Ⓓ Ⓔ
25 Ⓕ Ⓖ Ⓗ Ⓙ Ⓚ
26 Ⓐ Ⓑ Ⓒ Ⓓ Ⓔ
27 Ⓕ Ⓖ Ⓗ Ⓙ Ⓚ
28 Ⓐ Ⓑ Ⓒ Ⓓ Ⓔ
29 Ⓕ Ⓖ Ⓗ Ⓙ Ⓚ
30 Ⓐ Ⓑ Ⓒ Ⓓ Ⓔ
31 Ⓕ Ⓖ Ⓗ Ⓙ Ⓚ
32 Ⓐ Ⓑ Ⓒ Ⓓ Ⓔ
33 Ⓕ Ⓖ Ⓗ Ⓙ Ⓚ
34 Ⓐ Ⓑ Ⓒ Ⓓ Ⓔ
35 Ⓕ Ⓖ Ⓗ Ⓙ Ⓚ

# Answer Keys

## Reading/Language Arts Practice Test, Part 1

| | |
|---|---|
| 1. D | 11. C |
| 2. G | 12. J |
| 3. B | 13. A |
| 4. H | 14. G |
| 5. D | 15. D |
| 6. G | 16. F |
| 7. A | 17. C |
| 8. G | 18. J |
| 9. D | 19. A |
| 10. H | 20. H |

21. Answers may vary. Examples: They felt sad because it had not rained in 12 months. They were going to die.

22. Answers may vary. Examples: At first, they thought the pit was just a hole in the ground, or they did not understand what their dad was doing. At the end, they were amazed, or impressed.

23. Answers may vary. Example: Both stories involve characters who need water and find a way to obtain it. Both stories involve learning from nature.

24. Example:

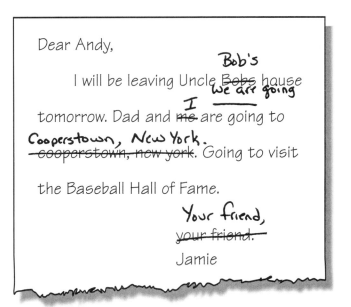

25. Answers will vary but should describe something the student learned. Example: I learned that you can find water in the desert.

# Reading/Language Arts
## Practice Test, Part 2

| | | | |
|---|---|---|---|
| 26. | G | 36. | G |
| 27. | A | 37. | D |
| 28. | J | 38. | F |
| 29. | B | 39. | C |
| 30. | H | 40. | J |
| 31. | C | 41. | C |
| 32. | F | 42. | G |
| 33. | D | 43. | D |
| 34. | H | 44. | F |
| 35. | B | 45. | B |

46. His goal was to fly solo around the world in a balloon.

47. Answers may vary. Example: He had to land in Asia because his oxygen system was not working properly.

48. Answers will vary. Example: She was training to live on *Mir*, a Russian space station, with two cosmonauts.

49. Example:

The first airplane flights ~~take~~ took place on December ~~17 1903~~ 17, 1903. Orville and ~~wilbur wright~~ Wilbur Wright made history that day in Kitty Hawk, ~~north~~ North ~~carolina~~ Carolina. Each man made two flights. The ~~most long~~ longest flight lasted 59 seconds.

50. Answers will vary but the response should give the student's preference of a hot-air balloon or the Space Shuttle, it should give a reason, and it should be written correctly.

# Mathematics
## Practice Test, Part 1

| | | | |
|---|---|---|---|
| 1. | C | 9. | A |
| 2. | F | 10. | F |
| 3. | B | 11. | B |
| 4. | J | 12. | J |
| 5. | E | 13. | B |
| 6. | H | 14. | G |
| 7. | C | 15. | C |
| 8. | J | | |

16. Answers will vary. Examples:
    (a) 3 quarters, 1 penny
    (b) 2 quarters, 2 dimes, 1 nickel, 1 penny
    (c) 2 quarters, 5 nickels, 1 penny

17. Answers will vary. Example: Glen bought 6 packs of baseball cards. There were 7 cards in each pack. How many cards did he buy in all?

18. Answers should match question 17. Example: 6 packs $\times$ 7 cards = 42 baseball cards.

19. 65,321

20. No, the odds are not the same because the area marked C is twice as large as A or B. Janice should make the three areas the same size. (Or some students might suggest that it would be easiest to divide C into two equal areas and label one C and one D.)

Scholastic Professional Books

**Mathematics**
**Practice Test, Part 2**

| | |
|---|---|
| 21. D | 29. A |
| 22. K | 30. G |
| 23. A | 31. C |
| 24. H | 32. G |
| 25. D | 33. B |
| 26. F | 34. H |
| 27. C | 35. D |
| 28. H | |

36. Answers will vary. Examples:
    6 adults and 22 children (6 × $4)
    + (22 × $2) = $68.00
    8 adults and 18 children (8 × $4)
    + (18 × $2) = $68.00

37. Answers will vary. By rounding to
    80 people × $5, the estimated total is $400.

38. 20 ft + 20 ft + 5 ft + 5 ft = 50 ft

39. Trish can make six different outfits, as shown in the tree diagram below.

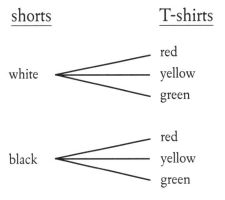

40. Example:

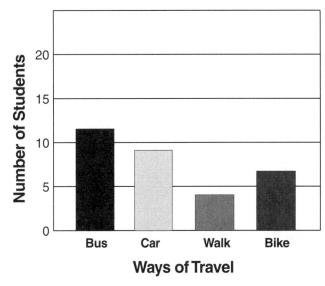

# Scoring Chart

**Student Name** _____ **Grade** _____

**Teacher Name** _____ **Date** _____

*Directions:* For each part of the test, count the number of questions answered correctly. Write the "Number Correct" in the box. To find the Percentage Score, divide the "Number Correct" by the "Total" number of questions. For example, 40 correct out of 50 questions = 40 ÷ 50, which is 0.8, or 80%.

|  | Number Correct/Total | Percentage Score |
|---|---|---|
| **Reading/Language Arts Practice Test** |  |  |
| Part 1: Questions 1–25 | /25 |  |
| Part 2: Questions 26–50 | /25 |  |
| Total Reading/Language Arts | /50 |  |
| **Mathematics Practice Test** |  |  |
| Part 1: Questions 1–20 | /20 |  |
| Part 2: Questions 21–40 | /20 |  |
| Total Mathematics | /40 |  |